Oxfordshire
Edited by Michelle Afford

First published in Great Britain in 2007 by:
Young Writers
Remus House
Coltsfoot Drive
Peterborough
PE2 9JX
Telephone: 01733 890066
Website: www.youngwriters.co.uk

All Rights Reserved

© *Copyright Contributors 2007*

SB ISBN 978-1 84431 098 2

Foreword

Young Writers was established in 1991 and has been passionately devoted to the promotion of reading and writing in children and young adults ever since. The quest continues today. Young Writers remains as committed to the nurturing of poetic and literary talent as ever.

This year's Young Writers competition has proven as vibrant and dynamic as ever and we are delighted to present a showcase of the best poetry from across the UK and in some cases overseas. Each poem has been selected from a wealth of *Little Laureates* entries before ultimately being published in this, our sixteenth primary school poetry series.

Once again, we have been supremely impressed by the overall quality of the entries we have received. The imagination, energy and creativity which has gone into each young writer's entry made choosing the poems a challenging and often difficult but ultimately hugely rewarding task - the general high standard of the work submitted ensured this opportunity to bring their poetry to a larger appreciative audience.

We sincerely hope you are pleased with this final collection and that you will enjoy *Little Laureates Oxfordshire* for many years to come.

Contents

Carswell Community Primary School
Emily Cackett (10)	1
Harry Doherty (11)	2
Toby Downes (10)	3
Birkan Dumanli (11)	4
Sean Fiddaman (10)	5
Katie Jane Horsfall (11)	6
Thomas Leaver (11)	7
Thomas Mullord (10)	8
Curtis Simmonds-Lee (10)	9
Lauren Barnes (10)	10

Carterton Primary School
Matthew Smith (9)	11
Emily Browne (9)	12
Molly Bishop (9)	13

Checkendon CE Primary School
Hannah Buckley (10)	14
Sam Cooke (9)	15
Elliot Glass (10)	16
Tim Davies (10)	17
Jasper Hughes (10)	18
Phoebe Gipson (9)	19
Joshua Allen (9)	20
Daisy Parker (11)	21
Daniel Cranstone (9)	22
Oliver Dodd (10)	23
Louise Allen (10)	24
Katie Shepherd (11)	25
Jennifer Clark (10)	26
Tom Smith (11)	27
Harry Wickens (10)	28
Kyri Roberts (10)	29
Rory Craven-Todd (9)	30
Keri Louise Allen (11)	31
Holly Price (10)	32
Kimberley Wise (9)	33
Alfie Clifton (9)	34

Nicole Bonner (10)	35
Georgia Rose Smith (10)	36

Longcot & Fernham Primary School

Jessica Davies (8)	37
Lucy Kent (8)	38
Hannah Jones (9)	39
Elle Simons (7)	40
Alex Warburton (9)	41
Josh Sheppard (7)	42
Holly Carlisle (8)	43
Alfie West (8)	44
George Timms (9)	45
Alicia Howe (8)	46

Marcham CE Primary School

Jasmine Skellington (8)	47
Briony Thomas (8)	48
Jordan Boseley (9)	49
Kirsty Preston (8)	50
Hannah French (9)	51
Dylan Hornsby (7)	52
Lawrence Mizen (8)	53
Katie Bell (9)	54
Amber Swain (9)	55
Ryan Fulton (10)	56
Jonathan Allison (7)	57
Louis Jackson (9)	58
Ciera Kent (9)	59
Kieran Mansbridge (8)	60
Kieran John Phillip Belcher (9)	61
Tervel Olinov Atanasov (9) & Johanna Wolff (8)	62

Orchard Close, Sibford School

Jake Mayo (12)	63
William Stroud (11)	64
Robert Macdonald (10)	65
Sean Hampson (11)	66
Madeline Fletcher (10)	67
Eric Foster-Smith (10)	68
Henry Moore (11)	69

Henry Wood (11)	70
Elliot Holland (10)	71
Hector Smith (11)	72
William Preece (10)	73
Scarlett Embury (11)	74
Kyle White (10)	75
Elizabeth Bradbury (11)	76

Orchard Fields Community School

Natalie Hardy (10)	77
Joe Booth (11)	78
Rhiannon Marchant (11)	79
Ricci Capel (11)	80
Chelsea Davis (10)	81
Taymar Lewis-Jones (9)	82
Katie Lea Trask (10)	83
Elloise Jones (9)	84
Alex Mason (9)	85
Liam Neil (10)	86
Lewis Foot (11)	87
Emily Braggins (10)	88
Sean Barnes (10)	89
Abrar Iqbal (10)	90
Joshua Barnes (9)	91
Nathan Blackman (11)	92
Kieran Holland (9)	93
Jarvis Marchant (11)	94
Lauren Ansell (10)	95
Georgia Smith (10)	96
Ellen Collett (11)	97
Tiffany Boisselle (10)	98
Saif Ali (11)	99
Thomas Tingley (10)	100
Andrew Penn (10)	101
Chelsea Coles (10)	102
Louise Buzzard (11)	103

Queen's Dyke Primary School

Ryan Clarke (11)	104
Umar Rashid (10)	105
Joe Simpson (10)	106

Sophie Minter (10)	107
Abbie Treleaven (10)	108
Eddie O'Sullivan (10)	109
Daniel Buckley (10)	110
Joshua Lathey (11)	111
Christian Olive (11)	112
Callum Clarke (11)	113
Rebecca Newport (10)	114
Ben Kinchin (11)	115
Owen Churchill (11)	116
Adina Gibbard (11)	117
Chloë Dunseath (11)	118
Ashley Ashcroft (11)	119
Sophie Wright (11)	120
Chloe Curtis (11)	121
Michael Long (11)	122
Kyle Frost (10)	123
Alicia Scammell (10)	124
Nick Morse (11)	125
Georgea Winstone (10)	126
Ashley Barnes (11)	127
Daisy Merriman (10)	128
Adam Field (10)	129
Chloe Lathey (11)	130
Mick Ritchie (10)	131
Chelsea Anderson (10)	132
Euan McGinness (10)	133
Liam Hole (10)	134
Callum MacDonald (10)	135
Ben Stanley (11)	136
Lewis Manning (10)	137
Ben Hardcastle (10)	138
Jordan Maycock (11)	139
Carlee Shayler (10)	140

Radley CE School

Nicholas Corrigan (7)	141
Daisy Stoyle (7)	142
Sebastian Charles Small (8)	143
Ryan Stubbs (8)	144
Samuel Yates (8)	145

Conor Mosedale (9)	146
Edward Walker (8)	147

St Mary's RC School, Bicester
Aoife Lyford (8)	148
Jacob Wise (8)	149
Ruth Anne Lazarus (8)	150

The Blake CE Primary School
Maddie Peacey (8)	152
Abigail Langley (8)	153
Oliver Moss (9)	154
Imogen Pitson (7)	155
Lewis Denbow (8)	156
Abbie Willcox (9)	157
Georgia Hackett (10)	158
Katie Steele (8)	159
Sebastian Ombler (7)	160
Freddie Greenan (7)	161
William Monahan (7)	162
Lucy Cox (8)	163
Charlotte Stoker (8)	164
Edward Woods (7)	165
Jack Booth (7)	166
Emily Chapman (8)	167
Thomas Alty (8)	168

West Kidlington Primary School
Leah Gray (11)	169
Naomi Heffer (10)	170

Wootton by Woodstock CE (Aided) Primary School
Joshua Reynolds (11)	171
Louis Williams (9)	172
Luke New (10)	173
William Honey (9)	174
Skye Radford (8)	175
Ben Capel (10)	176
Thomas Ramli-Davies (8)	177
Frank Robert New (8)	178

George Parker (8)	179
Finlay Mayo (8)	180
Joshua Ramli-Davies (10)	181
Henry Chesterman (7)	182
Peter Moss (9)	183
Megan Dyer (8)	184
Alexandra Cross (9)	185
Molly Capel (8)	186
Calla Cambrey (9)	187
Lucy Oliver (7)	188

The Poems

'A'

Tiny toddler
Leaf lover
Warm wrapper
Cocoon breaker
World waker
Wing shaker
Lovely flyer
Nectar eater
Beauty finder
So that means a
Butterfly!

Emily Cackett (10)
Carswell Community Primary School

The Wondrous Animal

Flame keeper
High-flyer
Mini volcano
Never dies
Ash-born
Wonder bird
Beautifully amazing . . .

Phoenix.

Harry Doherty (11)
Carswell Community Primary School

Wolves - Haiku

Beyond the tall trees
The wolves gather in their pack
In the bright full moon.

Toby Downes (10)
Carswell Community Primary School

There Was A Teacher

There was a teacher called Mrs Dyer
One day she had a flat tyre
She was late for school
She broke the rules
Oh, that poor Mrs Dyer!

Birkan Dumanli (11)
Carswell Community Primary School

My Dog Called Alfie - Cinquain

Alfie
Chocolate dog
Playful and exciting
Always dirty and destructive
Mental.

Sean Fiddaman (10)
Carswell Community Primary School

A Kennings Poem

Paper fetcher
Loyal companion
Postman chaser
Bone digger
Intruder alarmer
Meat eater
Sausage stealer
Park racer
Flea monster
Ankle nipper
. . . a dog!

Katie Jane Horsfall (11)
Carswell Community Primary School

The White Dolphin

There was a white dolphin called Bob
Who ate purple corn on the cob
He could drive motor cars
And bend metal bars
That mighty white dolphin called Bob.

Thomas Leaver (11)
Carswell Community Primary School

There Once Was An Old Farmer Bob

There once was an old farmer Bob
Who really liked to do his job
Best farmer in the land
Sold the best kind of brand
What an intelligent man, Bob.

Thomas Mullord (10)
Carswell Community Primary School

The Flying Thing

Fire breather
Killing beast
Fast flyer
Massive teeth
Bad breath
Long tail
Gigantic claws
A dragon.

Curtis Simmonds-Lee (10)
Carswell Community Primary School

There Was A Girl Called Holly

There was a nice girl called Holly
Who had a nice friend called Polly
Holly was nice and helpful
Made of sugar and spice, never hurtful
That nice girl called Holly!

Lauren Barnes (10)
Carswell Community Primary School

Football

My name is Matthew,
My age is nine,
I like to play football all the time,
I play at night, I play in the day,
I'll play the first team on Saturday,
My dream is to win,
My dream is to score,
With my mum on the sideline
Ready to roar,
One day I will meet Rooney and play by his side,
Together we'll win for England, the cup and our pride.

Matthew Smith (9)
Carterton Primary School

A River Called Tawton

On a river called Tawton
That ran through Bourton
Floated a duck called Mary
'Is that really necessary?'
She said to her brother John
Who was dragging her out of River Tawton
'Yes it is,' said her brother
'Because the alligator mother
Is coming straight for us
And she definitely saw us.'
'Oh,' said Mary
'She's very scary.'
'So get a move on
Or we'll be eaten on River Tawton.'
'Boo hoo,' said Mother
'Maybe I should try for another
Because I've just lost my children
Oh, darling Ken
What should I do?
Boo hoo, boo hoo!'

Emily Browne (9)
Carterton Primary School

Never Go Near A Crocodile

Never go near a crocodile, or it might suddenly bite,
Never go near a crocodile, it'll make you shout with fright.

Never go near a crocodile, or it might shake its tail,
Never go near a crocodile, it'll make you start to wail.

Never go near a crocodile, it might come near you,
Never go near a crocodile, or you need to shout, *'Boo!'*

Molly Bishop (9)
Carterton Primary School

London

London is a hummingbird,
Humming noisily,
Busily moving,
Its beauty growing by the hour,
As bright and cheerful colours,
Swirl around.

A romantic moon,
Shines on the Thames,
Making the water,
A million diamonds glinting.

Hannah Buckley (10)
Checkendon CE Primary School

Paris At Night

Paris is a mime artist
Painting dreams in the air
Romance floats in the water
All is quiet
Until
The fireworks crash
Filling the air
With light and sound
Then
Finally
The city sleeps
Only an old road sweeper
Moves slowly, silently
Through the dark roads.

Sam Cooke (9)
Checkendon CE Primary School

Brighton

Brighton is a playful puppy,
Full of enjoyment and fun.
Ever entertaining,
Never boring or lazy.
Its cheerful face lights up the country
And amazes everyone.
Brighton is a playful puppy,
Noisy, expensive and full of life.

Brighton at night is a fat cat, lounging by the fire,
Relaxed and very much laid back.
It's so peaceful and quiet,
Although it's evilly black.
Sometimes you'll hear it snoring,
A car rolling down the street.
Too rich, proud and well-fed,
Looking forward to a nice comfy bed.

Elliot Class (10)
Checkendon CE Primary School

Carlisle

Out of the night-time fog looms,
A Minotaur of a castle,
Roaming a labyrinth of dark streets and alleyways.
The *swish, swish, swish* of the road sweeper,
Is the Minotaur's tail brushing on the pavement.
The *clop, clop, clop* of a policeman's boots,
The Minotaur's hooves on the cobbles
And a roar from the occasional car,
The yellow eyes on tall metal antennae finally close.

Day returns,
Happiness arrives,
The city is the River Eden.
Always the same, yet different.
From monsters to minnows,
A shoal of colour and noise,
Flickering, darting, weaving in and out.
The cars and lorries are the otters,
Searching for food
A continuous hunt.

Tim Davies (10)
Checkendon CE Primary School

Paris

Paris is a bumblebee,
Brightly coloured,
Buzzing with people talking and shouting to each other,
The Eiffel Tower is a sting,
Pointing up to the sky,
Exciting sights and smells and colours swirl around everywhere,
The city's wings beat,
Creating a cool wind that mixes all the colours
Into a mix of spilt paint,
Splattered on the floor and still wet.

At night, Paris is a firefly,
Twinkling with lights as the sun goes down,
Still quietly buzzing with activity as people go home,
Gradually darkening
As midnight draws near.

Jasper Hughes (10)
Checkendon CE Primary School

Somewhere In The City

New York is a silent shadow
Creeping slowly through the quiet night,
Never sleeping,
Never dying,
Always alive.
New York is a shop,
Full of happy, smiling people,
Busy, chatting,
Laughing, crying,
Living their lives.

Phoebe Gipson (9)
Checkendon CE Primary School

Tiger Eyes

The city at night screams
The eyes of tigers run through the streets
Terrifying
The moonlight is bright
Blinding
The snake river
Slivers through the darkness
Hissing.

Joshua Allen (9)
Checkendon CE Primary School

My City

Tokyo is a yellow flower
Turning its face to the sun.
The tall buildings are stems
Stretching up toward the sky.

Tokyo is a hummingbird
Brightly coloured
Wings beating fast.

Tokyo is a garden
With wonderful things inside.

Daisy Parker (11)
Checkendon CE Primary School

My City

My city is a black dog
Dark, dingy and mysterious
Big and hungry
The streets bark noisily
Alive with people shouting
The buildings are legs
Strong and heavy
Silent and still.

Daniel Cranstone (9)
Checkendon CE Primary School

London At Sunset

The Thames lit up by the sun at sunset
Is a dragon's flame
Lighting the way
The people of the city
Buzz and the shadows of bees
Creep along the walls
There is darkness
And spiders scurry on the floor
Swans skim the surface of the water
White boats heading for the banks.

Oliver Dodd (10)
Checkendon CE Primary School

The City

My city is a sewing box,
With glorious things inside.
The coloured threads,
Are the quiet roads.
The sparkling
Needles and pins,
Are blades of grass sticking out of the garden.
The city is a patchwork
Of coloured fabrics,
All joined together.

Louise Allen (10)
Checkendon CE Primary School

My City

My city is a yellow rose
Standing proudly in the sun.
The golden bricks of buildings shine
The beautiful petals of the bright lights
Gleam in the evening city.

Katie Shepherd (11)
Checkendon CE Primary School

London

London is a saucepan,
The wonderful scent of happiness
Dances through the air.
The pouring of shopping bags
Goes round and round the city.
When the secret ingredient of visitors comes,
The houses and parks come to life.
All these wonderful things
Put together, make
The flowing soup of excitement.

Jennifer Clark (10)
Checkendon CE Primary School

My City

Rome is a tiger,
Always awake,
Eyes that never close,
Its bright colours stripe the streets,
While inside it is dark and cold,
Lonely and desolate,
With no colour or feeling at all.
The city hunts its prey,
Slinking down the curving alleyways,
Prowling the famous monuments,
Until the sun flames bright.

Tom Smith (11)
Checkendon CE Primary School

The City

The city is a deadly viper
Hiding in the dark night
Simply waiting to strike.
Walking around outside
You'll hear its deathly quiet.
Beware of the shadow
Which appears around the corner.
Don't turn around
Don't make a sound.

Harry Wickens (10)
Checkendon CE Primary School

Prague

Prague is a sewing box
Full of hidden treasures
The colourful lights
Are multicoloured cotton reels
The taxis are needles
Of yellow thread
Weaving in and out
Of the afternoon traffic
A ribbon of water
Winds through the humming city.

Kyri Roberts (10)
Checkendon CE Primary School

Shadow City

Paris at night is a shadow city,
Creeping quietly and mysteriously,
Waiting for the day.
The Tower is a giant hunter,
Hunting the city down,
Ready to pounce.
The tree shadows guard the city,
The buildings watch over the people
Protectively.
The moon is a glowing ball of brightness,
Which lights up the river's surface,
Curling the broken reflections,
Paris at night is a shadow city.

Rory Craven-Todd (9)
Checkendon CE Primary School

My City

My city is a monster
Its darkness fades the light.
The devil rats creep in and out
Of the dirty, deserted restaurants.
Yellow eyes watch
As the streets sleep.
Monstrous breath blows
Along alleyways
Rustling old wrappers around corners.

Keri Louise Allen (11)
Checkendon CE Primary School

My City

My city is a black cat
That prowls the dark night,
A dark place filled with
The howls of cars
Its headlamp eyes
Watch the black streets.

Holly Price (10)
Checkendon CE Primary School

Paris

Paris is a patchwork quilt
Of many different colours
A giant needle
Sews the silver ribbon of river
Through the city
Sequin fireworks fall
Through the dark sky
Filling the summer air
With sparkles of coloured light.

Kimberley Wise (9)
Checkendon CE Primary School

My City

My city is a black cat
With its fur sweeping
Against the buildings
At night
Quiet
As it stalks its prey
While the cars purr
Along the dark streets.

Alfie Clifton (9)
Checkendon CE Primary School

Somewhere In The City

A bright day in London
Is a hummingbird
Beauty outstanding
Amazing colours swirl
Around.

An evening in London
Is a romantic red rose
The moon glinting on the Thames
The cooling breeze
The colours under the street lamps
As bright as daylight.

Nicole Bonner (10)
Checkendon CE Primary School

Somewhere In The City

My city at night is an eerie sound,
A soft *swish . . . swish . . .*
Interrupted by stampedes of cars,
Screaming drunks, shouting sellers,
Dusty, rustling, cold.
Then quiet again,
Swish . . . swish . . .
An eerie sound,
A city crying to be loved.

Georgia Rose Smith (10)
Checkendon CE Primary School

Journey Across A Stormy Sea

Crashing waves
Guide me
Shining lighthouse
Let me see the sharp rocks
Banging rocks
Move out of my way
Snapping sharks
Help me
Howling wind
Calm me down
Flashing fish
Help me eat
Making nothing happen
Lead me to the hidden island.

Jessica Davies (8)
Longcot & Fernham Primary School

Purple

Purple is my favourite colour
Purple like the glistening lavender
Swaying and shining in the sun.

Purple as the bright lilac sitting in the flower bed
And swishing in the wind.

Purple like sparkly mauve on the little girl's top
That I see on telly.

Lucy Kent (8)
Longcot & Fernham Primary School

Journey Through Space

Shining stars
Guide me,
Shimmering moon
Hear me,
Huge planets
Protect me,
Enormous spaceship
Help me,
Bright sun
Fear me,
Green Earth
Find me,
Lead me to my landing spot.

Hannah Jones (9)
Longcot & Fernham Primary School

Journey Through Space

Glittering stars,
Guide me,
Firing rockets,
Carry me,
Spinning planets,
Protect me,
Chatting astronauts,
Save me,
Talking aliens,
Guide me,
Shining moon,
Save me,
Lead me back to Earth.

Elle Simons (7)
Longcot & Fernham Primary School

Flashing Rockets

Flashing rockets,
Hear me,
Speeding asteroids,
See me,
Shining stars,
Guide me,
Spinning planets,
Miss me,
Jumping astronauts,
Help me,
Scary aliens,
Leave me,
Guide me to safe Saturn.

Alex Warburton (9)
Longcot & Fernham Primary School

Blue

Blue is my favourite colour
Blue is like the blue shimmering sea
When I go to France.
Blue as your veins
That carry blood in your body.
Blue like a blueberry
On a prickly bush
That I eat on Wednesdays.
Blue as a glowing diamond
In a jewel box.
Blue as the hottest
Summer sky.

Josh Sheppard (7)
Longcot & Fernham Primary School

Journey Through Space

Soaring rocket
Carry me,
Twinkling stars
Calm me,
Spinning planets
Guide me,
Talking aliens
Protect me,
Rocky asteroid belt
Guard me,
Lead me back to Earth.

Holly Carlisle (8)
Longcot & Fernham Primary School

Blue

Blue is my favourite colour
Blue as the sparkling dolphin swimming in the sea
Blue like the dark cars going across the motorway
Blue as the bright blue sky while aeroplanes fly across it
Blue as people's glazing eyes while looking at paintings
Blue like the sparkling sharks swimming in the sea.

Alfie West (8)
Longcot & Fernham Primary School

Space

Flashing space shuttle,
Guide me,
Jumping aliens,
Help me,
Floating astronaut,
Spot me,
Metamorphic rock,
See me,
Booming Red Devils,
Save me,
Glittering stars,
Light my way,
Lead me to safe Saturn!

George Timms (9)
Longcot & Fernham Primary School

Journey Across The Stormy Sea

Snapping sharks,
Calm me
Bubbling fish,
Feed me
Bumpy rock,
Guide me
Crashing thunder,
Help me
Lightning bashing,
Rock me
Wild sealife,
Hear me
Lead me to an island.

Alicia Howe (8)
Longcot & Fernham Primary School

Fairies

Fairies glitter in the snow
Always making fairies glow.
Summer sun warms up their wings
Always making fairies sing.
Fairies flying up so high
Lighting up the winter sky.
So they really think they can do it
Oh yes, they do, so let's get to it!

Jasmine Skellington (8)
Marcham CE Primary School

Cats And Kittens

Fluffy cats, cuddly kittens
All in their cute white mittens.
They eat birds, they eat spiders
But most of all, they love tigers.
They would like to fly with birds
They don't like to swim in the sea
But most of all, they like you and me.
They jump up high onto fences
And they can perform their own defences.
My cats attack dogs, oh yes, they really do
But most of all, (I don't like to do this)
I have to clean up their number twos.
When my cats had their kittens
They were really funny
And when I played with them
They wriggled on my tummy.

Briony Thomas (8)
Marcham CE Primary School

Spies

Spies, spies, secret spies
Love to shoot and love to hide
They spy on you and on me
Will I ever be free?
Spies, spies, spies
Will they ever learn not to hide?

Jordan Boseley (9)
Marcham CE Primary School

Bratz

Bratz are nice
Bratz are pretty
They have sparkles in their eyes
Rock angels are like diamonds
That twinkle in the sky

My Bratz dolls are special to me
I play with them every day
I dress them up and put on their shoes
So I can play with them all day

My Bratz dolls have a stage to play on
And they can dance
And they can dance
To their favourite song
I have different CDs to dance to
So we can dance all day long!

Kirsty Preston (8)
Marcham CE Primary School

Big Cats

Big cats hunting up the trees
Drinking water from the streams
Babies snoozing and having tea
Oh my gosh they're scaring me!
Running so fast through the forest
Big cats are attacking prey
They fight with their claws
And scare things away
And also they reign every day
Leaping over fire, everybody cheering
Throwing things and laughing
And crowding round to take pictures
The big cats are guarding their prey
And scaring things away.

Hannah French (9)
Marcham CE Primary School

Dragons

Dragons, dragons,
In the sky
Like an eagle really high.
Dragons, dragons,
Blowing fire
To keep them warm in the cold.
Dragons, dragons,
In the sky
Blowing fire on the clouds in the night.
Dragons, dragons,
Big and strong
And they have a big tail.

Dylan Hornsby (7)
Marcham CE Primary School

Dragon Rider, Dragon Rider

Dragon Rider, Dragon Rider
Powerful and rough
Dragon Rider, Dragon Rider
Angry and tough
Dragon Rider, Dragon Rider
Spooky and fast
Dragon Rider, Dragon Rider
Super and brave
Dragon Rider, Dragon Rider
Really strong
Dragon Rider, Dragon Rider
Really dirty
Dragon Rider, Dragon Rider
So smart
Dragon Rider, Dragon Rider
Always saves the day.

Lawrence Mizen (8)
Marcham CE Primary School

Hamsters

Golden hamsters, they crawl everywhere
Listen to everything all day long
They eat from bowls and drink out of bottles
They love to run
Funny hamsters crawl on people's hands
Do you like hamsters?
I do!

Katie Bell (9)
Marcham CE Primary School

There Was A Young Lady From France

There was a young lady from France
Who was desperate to learn to dance
And she had a black cat
Which was extremely fat
That poor young lady from France.

Amber Swain (9)
Marcham CE Primary School

There Was An Old Man

There was an old man called Dan
Who wanted a brand new pan
So he begged for money
But instead got honey
So Dan got hit with a pan.

Ryan Fulton (10)
Marcham CE Primary School

Rugby

Rugby, rugby, rough rugby
Rough people getting hurt
Rugby, rugby, rough rugby
Happy sport
Rugby, rugby, rough rugby
The men kicking the ball
Rugby, rugby, rough rugby
Big and bigger cuts
Rugby, rugby, rough rugby
Smiles and kicks
Rugby, rugby, rough rugby
Cheers and big cuddles
Rugby, rugby, rough rugby
Kicks over the bar
Rugby, rugby, rough rugby.

Jonathan Allison (7)
Marcham CE Primary School

There Was A Keeper In A Zoo

There was a keeper in a zoo
Cleaning up some rhino poo
There was a tiger in a tree
Lifting its leg to do a pee
Poor old keeper in the zoo!

Louis Jackson (9)
Marcham CE Primary School

There Was An Old Man Who Liked To Sing

There was an old man who liked to sing
Who thought he had really big wings
One day be bought a small kitten
Who chewed on his mitten
The poor old man who liked to sing.

Ciera Kent (9)
Marcham CE Primary School

There Was An Old Man With His Cat

There was an old man with his cat
Who ran away with his hat
He kicked a tree
And broke his knee
That silly old man with a cat.

Kieran Mansbridge (8)
Marcham CE Primary School

There Was An Old Man From Leeds

There was an old man from Leeds
Who bought a car with some bees
He got honey
But instead he wanted money
That poor old man from Leeds.

Kieran John Phillip Belcher (9)
Marcham CE Primary School

There Was An Old Man With A Pig

There was an old man with a pig
Who went out to the fields to dig
He took a banana
And went to a farmer
And he got a pound for his pig.

Tervel Olinov Atanasov (9) & Johanna Wolff (8)
Marcham CE Primary School

Hedgehogs

The hedgehog's born in the summer night
All alone - sad and frightened.
The winter dawns, cold and icy
'Let's gather food to store up our nests.'
Comfy leaves to lie on
To curl up in a spiky ball
For the stormy nights in darkness.

Jake Mayo (12)
Orchard Close, Sibford School

Sleepless Night

In the night, I woke up
I just laid there
Listening to the sounds outside
Trees whistled
Foxes growled
Stars glowed.

William Stroud (11)
Orchard Close, Sibford School

The Gannet

The gannet out of its nest again
Desperate to feed its young one
Up in the air above the cliffs
Then the signal -
It swoops into the saltiness of the sea
Out with a fish
The chick gulps it down
The gannet flies away
Leaving the baby
Alone.

Robert Macdonald (10)
Orchard Close, Sibford School

The Man

Deep in your mind, there's a man
This man is your mind
He is everything
Every time I say this, the man gets closer
Because day is night
Our eyes drop
You are sleeping
The man is here
Will it be good or bad?
It's the man.

Sean Hampson (11)
Orchard Close, Sibford School

Daydreamer

Fluffy marshmallow clouds
A garden with a gate
Your lesson is far away
Birds whispering
Drinking cool water from the fountain
A house in the distance, its chimney smoking
A rabbit hops into your arms
Sweetness in the air
Trees dressed in pink blossom
Slowly, you're coming back
To life.

Madeline Fletcher (10)
Orchard Close, Sibford School

The Sorrow Man

His deep dark eyes were burning through my heart
His face was as black as night
His clothes, ragged and torn
He had a little top hat and half of it was gone
Then he saw me
And scurried away, into the dank alley.

Eric Foster-Smith (10)
Orchard Close, Sibford School

Cocker Spaniel - Kennings

Game seeker
Bed warmer
Newspaper pulveriser
Scent catcher
Fowl retriever
Family protector.

Henry Moore (11)
Orchard Close, Sibford School

Cocker Spaniels - Haikus

Happy and playful
Always full of energy
Restless and cheerful

Always friendly dogs
Never grumpy, always kind
Always different.

Henry Wood (11)
Orchard Close, Sibford School

Rabbit

Tall fluffy ears
Lovely brown eyes
Spiky thin whiskers
Munching carrots all day long
Sitting in a cage
Waiting till I come home.

Elliot Holland (10)
Orchard Close, Sibford School

My Cats Kennings

Machine purrers
Rodent wreckers
Food lovers
Milk lappers
Furry sleepers
Seat warmers
Attention seekers
AGA companions.

Hector Smith (11)
Orchard Close, Sibford School

My Dog Kennings

Barking blaster
Football player
Joy bringer
Family lover
Happiness creator
Sadness taker
Food muncher
Water leaver
Rain hater
Muscle builder
Family protector
Ball chaser
Daytime sleeper
Rapid runner
Vet loather
Cat detester
Friend former.

William Preece (10)
Orchard Close, Sibford School

The Sea And The Sky

Gentle waves flowing like the wind
Beautiful seaweed bobbing across the water
Multicoloured fish swimming down below
Lying in a boat, looking at the summer sky
A single cloud catches my eye
Floating like the sea across the air
Then I fall asleep, happily lying there.

Scarlett Embury (11)
Orchard Close, Sibford School

Cat

Mouse catcher
Long sleeper
Food guzzler
Witch petter
Unlucky charmer
Bed stealer
Morning alarmer
Bird terroriser
Affection seeker.

Kyle White (10)
Orchard Close, Sibford School

My Rabbit

Food grabber
Fussy eater
Escape artist
House explorer
Finger sniffer
Carrot cruncher
Nose twitcher
Tall sound catcher.

Elizabeth Bradbury (11)
Orchard Close, Sibford School

My Rat Dad
(In the style of 'My Sparrow Gran' by Berlie Doherty)

My rat dad
Is the smelly one
Taking and eating
And a pink wet nose
He squeaks and squeals
He eats off the floor
That fills his big belly
And when morning comes
When he has scurried enough
I give him his mug
While giving him a hug
That is hairy and spiky.

Natalie Hardy (10)
Orchard Fields Community School

My Snail Friend
(In the style of 'My Sparrow Gran' by Berlie Doherty)

My snail friend,
My friend, the football one,
He's so naughty,
Slow and so small,
He's just a centimetre tall,
He is so slimy,
My snail friend,
Has long hair
And looks like a bear,
He is so nice,
But he's not worth the price,
He rolls the dice,
He's my snail friend.

Joe Booth (11)
Orchard Fields Community School

My Lion Brother
(In the style of 'My Sparrow Gran' by Berlie Doherty)

My lion brother
Is the protective one
Tall and fast
To get the work done
He's bright, brown-eyed
He's got a lot of hair on his head
He eats a lot
That's what he said
At night he's sly and brave to catch his prey
That's what you get
At my brother's age.

Rhiannon Marchant (11)
Orchard Fields Community School

My Mouse Friend
(In the style of 'My Sparrow Gran' by Berlie Doherty)

My mouse friend
Is the naughty one
Loud and noisy
Quick and made of brick,
He loves to have a laugh
And loves to be daft,
He has a tail like a rope
But he does not use soap,
He has a big belly
Which is very smelly,
Even though he's a mouse
He has a very large house.

Ricci Capel (11)
Orchard Fields Community School

My Monkey Sister
(In the style of 'My Sparrow Gran' by Berlie Doherty)

My monkey sister
Is the dangling one
Swaying and swaying
With brown cheeky eyes
She swings from her bed
She swings up trees
She whacks her head
When she gets out of bed
When evening comes.

Chelsea Davis (10)
Orchard Fields Community School

My Horse Mum
(In the style of 'My Sparrow Gran' by Berlie Doherty)

My horse mum
Is the charging around one
She never stops
With blue eyes
She's the pretty one
She is the energetic and slim one
She is always busy and listens
She takes care of herself
And is very gentle
She has short dark brown hair
Always laughing and smiling
She is the best mum in the world!

Taymar Lewis-Jones (9)
Orchard Fields Community School

My Dog Dad
(In the style of 'My Sparrow Gran' by Berlie Doherty)

My dog dad
Is the running one
Lazy and fat
And dark-haired
He charges and barks
He begs and growls
He ruins the towels
He's always busy
And when evening comes
He snuggles in his bed
That's very warm
And off to sleep he goes.

Katie Lea Trask (10)
Orchard Fields Community School

My Cheetah Nan
(In the style of 'My Sparrow Gran' by Berlie Doherty)

My cheetah nan
Is the chatty one
Smoothly and steadily
And bright blue-eyed
She roars and is intelligent
She will hurry and be quick
I'll sit on her lap
Snug in her arms
That are extremely warm
My nan cheetah is very calm.

Elloise Jones (9)
Orchard Fields Community School

My Hyena Friend
(In the style of 'My Sparrow Gran' by Berlie Doherty)

My hyena friend,
Likes to have a laugh,
He jumps up and down,
Into the bath!
My hyena friend,
Is the hairy one,
Even though
He likes to add up sums!
My hyena friend,
Is the chosen one,
Even though
He always likes fun!
My hyena friend,
Is the reading one,
Even though,
He likes the sun!

Alex Mason (9)
Orchard Fields Community School

My Cat Mum
(In the style of 'My Sparrow Gran' by Berlie Doherty)

My cat mum
Is the super one
Jumping up and down
Having fun
Helping everyone
She keeps everything tidy
Just for me and you
She is intelligent
Smiley, caring
Really helpful and she never stops
Loving you
She has bright, beautiful blue eyes.

Liam Neil (10)
Orchard Fields Community School

My Monkey Dad
(In the style of 'My Sparrow Gran' by Berlie Doherty)

My monkey dad
Is very, very hairy
But sometimes acts like a fairy
And can also be a bit scary
He is pretty strong
Looking after everyone
Even though he weighs a ton
He has the biggest belly
And is a little bit smelly
Sometimes can be loud
But makes a good sound
And I am still proud
To have a dad like this
I wouldn't give him a miss!

Lewis Foot (11)
Orchard Fields Community School

My Cat Mum
(In the style of 'My Sparrow Gran' by Berlie Doherty)

My cat mum
Is snuggly and warm
She loves to pounce
She's the brave one
She's grey like the sky
On a rainy day
She's really speedy
She's bright green-eyed
I snuggle in her arms
All snug and warm
She creeps around the house
She is really mad
She slides through doors.

Emily Braggins (10)
Orchard Fields Community School

My Tortoise Dad
(In the style of 'My Sparrow Gran' by Berlie Doherty)

My tortoise dad
He munches on cakes
He's quite fat
He moans a lot
He's very slow
He's really lazy
Not very brainy
Watches telly
Drinks beer
And when my mum shouts
His head disappears!

Sean Barnes (10)
Orchard Fields Community School

My Monkey Friend
(In the style of 'My Sparrow Gran' by Berlie Doherty)

My monkey friend
Is the jumpy one
That likes hockey
And is speedy
But is really greedy
He likes playing football
Never lets anyone else play
He is always happy
And has a lot of junk
But has no energy to run
And stays in front of the TV
And never gets up.

Abrar Iqbal (10)
Orchard Fields Community School

My Lion Brother
(In the style of 'My Sparrow Gran' by Berlie Doherty)

My lion brother
Is the brave one
Strong and powerful
With sharp yellow teeth
He prowls and growls
He runs and charges
He rolls his brown eyes
And stares in the sky
He lays on his bed
And goes to sleep
He brings me his book
And lays on my chest.

Joshua Barnes (9)
Orchard Fields Community School

My Gorilla Mum
(In the style of 'My Sparrow Gran' by Berlie Doherty)

My gorilla mum
Is big and funny
She goes bananas
When I don't do my homework
She has good eyesight
She can see me from miles away
She grooms me when I sit on her lap
Good at gripping
Never lets go
She is very brainy
Helps me to solve problems
She's a loving, lovely, likeable person
She loves to sit and watch TV
Her favourite programme is the banana one
She climbs around the house
After TV and eats the bugs
And fruit she finds on her way
Beware of my snugly, warm mum.

Nathan Blackman (11)
Orchard Fields Community School

My Lion Dad
(In the style of 'My Sparrow Gran' by Berlie Doherty)

My strong dad
Has strong claws
He munches on zebra
He jumps into the bushes
He clambers onto the prey
Chews them
Then he comes home
I jump onto his back
And go *boo!*

Kieran Holland (9)
Orchard Fields Community School

My Wolf Dad
(In the style of 'My Sparrow Gran' by Berlie Doherty)

My wolf dad
A hunting one
Spectacular and outstanding
And dark-eyed
He howls, wolf-like
A mysterious prowler hunting
And a dashing, brutal beast
When the morning sun rises
My dad is glad
Because he gets to put
His snug arms around me
To wake me up.

Jarvis Marchant (11)
Orchard Fields Community School

My Squirrel Mum
(In the style of 'My Sparrow Gran' by Berlie Doherty)

My squirrel mum
Is the swinging one
Digs all day then eats all night
With her wide eyes gleaming in the night
She scurries and scampers in a rush
She's the clever one
She always does the housework
She cares for all
She always helps people
My mum takes me on adventures
Just like good mums should
When evening comes upon us
I snuggle up with her fur-down-warm.

Lauren Ansell (10)
Orchard Fields Community School

My Swan Mum
(In the style of 'My Sparrow Gran' by Berlie Doherty)

My swan mum
Is the great, graceful one
Ruffling her beautiful feathers
Bright, shiny blue eyes
She is the alert one
When her work is over
She asks me if my homework is done
I sit on her lap and cuddle her
In her fluffy, feather-like arms.

Georgia Smith (10)
Orchard Fields Community School

My Skunk Dad
(In the style of 'My Sparrow Gran' by Berlie Doherty)

My skunk dad
Is the smelly one
Tidy and busy
And big, blue-eyed
He runs and raps
He picks up his fragments
That crowd his shelter
When night comes
And all is silent
He cooks me tea
And sits down
With his furry black arms around me
So beware of the smell master!

Ellen Collett (11)
Orchard Fields Community School

My Swan Nan
(In the style of 'My Sparrow Gran' by Berlie Doherty)

My swan nan
Is the beautiful one.
She is clean and colourful
Sometimes very harmless,
But if you are nasty to her
She will hiss horribly.
She keeps her head up high
When things are getting tough.
She makes sure I don't wander off
When she picks me up from school,
She talks softly
And hugs me warmly
In her white wings.

Tiffany Boisselle (10)
Orchard Fields Community School

My Tigress Mum
(In the style of 'My Sparrow Gran' by Berlie Doherty)

My tigress mum
She has sparkly eyes that glow with the Earth
Roars like there's no tomorrow
Fetches food like mad
Hunts and protects me
She idolises me with her fur
Yawns so you can see her sharp teeth
After she's finished her work
I run to her arms
So she reads me a story
While I go to sleep
When I cuddle into her arms
I'd better be aware of her claws.

Saif Ali (11)
Orchard Fields Community School

My Giraffe Brother
(In the style of 'My Sparrow Gran' by Berlie Doherty)

My giraffe brother
Tall and slow
Has got lots of light brown in his eyes
He likes the hot light
And he's happy and tall
He goes to school
And when he comes home
He sits and watches the telly
Then he goes to bed and goes to sleep.

Thomas Tingley (10)
Orchard Fields Community School

My Giraffe Gran
(In the style of 'My Sparrow Gran' by Berlie Doherty)

My giraffe gran
Is tall and slow
Is quiet and happy and smiles
My gran is tall
And slow and she is quiet
And happy and smiley.

Andrew Penn (10)
Orchard Fields Community School

My Fox Brother
(In the style of 'My Sparrow Gran' by Berlie Doherty)

My fox brother
Is the sly one
He creeps and sneaks
Tiptoes and steals
But is classy and clever
He lazes all day and waits until midnight
For his prey
Stealing biscuits from the tin
And hunting to find the chocolate
With his bright eyes
Howling and screaming at me.

Chelsea Coles (10)
Orchard Fields Community School

My Tiger Mum
(In the style of 'My Sparrow Gran' by Berlie Doherty)

Is a big softie
She growls at me when I do something wrong
And she cooks a big Sunday dinner
Every Sunday she cooks meat like a tiger
She's big, big like a cat
She flies around to do her housework
She always is busy like a tiger
And I can't believe my eyes
Lots of fur just like my mum.

Louise Buzzard (11)
Orchard Fields Community School

Cinquains

Morning
Stone Farm today
Very excited now
Now go to school, kiss family
My life

Midday
We're very close
Now have a look around
Go to dorms, unpack bags today
My week

Evening
Try their good food
Into dorms, now get changed
Have time to read a book or game
Goodnight

Next day
National walk
Cuts and bruises from rocks
Up and down hills is quite tiring
Swimming.

Ryan Clarke (11)
Queen's Dyke Primary School

The Boy From Our School

There once was a boy from our school
Whose hair was exceptionally cool
Spiky and pink
It made people think
Does he realise he looks like a fool?

Umar Rashid (10)
Queen's Dyke Primary School

A Boy From Our School

There was a boy from our school
Who liked dancing in the hall
His voice was so loud
He burst a cloud
That fool from our school.

Joe Simpson (10)
Queen's Dyke Primary School

Coming And Going To Stone Farm - Haikus

Monday
Wake up, time to go
It is Stone Farm week today
Goodbye Mum, see you

Tuesday
Splashing the water
Laughing and having fun there
Back to the farm now

Wednesday
Having a campfire
Lots and lots of marshmallows
Going to bed now

Thursday
Going to the dance
Getting ready for the dance
Doing the dance now

Friday
Packing my bags now
Saying bye to animals
Going home to Mum.

Sophie Minter (10)
Queen's Dyke Primary School

The Frost

The frost glistens upon the hard ground,
She looks like a silver shining pound,
Her fantastic glitter makes the earth shine,
She glitters in a nice neat line,
She gets scattered, scattered, scattered by Mr Frost,
There's so much of her I think she might be lost!

Her white sprinkle may make you blind,
But I'm sure it will also make you unwind,
Her wintry season will say goodbye
Hope you enjoyed this poem, time to fly!

Abbie Treleaven (10)
Queen's Dyke Primary School

Stone Farm - Cinquains

Morning
Get up
It's time to go
I will be strong and brave
I just can't wait, I am fearless
But scared

Leaving
Go now
Bye animals
I do not want to leave
Hello family, friends, sad now
But warm.

Eddie O'Sullivan (10)
Queen's Dyke Primary School

Volcano

I'm a volcano
Tall in the sky
Why do people fear me
And wish I'd die?

I'm the kindest thing here
And it's not a lie

So please don't fear me
And wish I'd die

Because I may be big
I may be brown
But there's no need to hate me
And make me crash down!

Daniel Buckley (10)
Queen's Dyke Primary School

The Bumble Dropper Kennings

A bumble dropper
A lettuce lover
A seed cruncher
A carrot muncher
A vet hater
A lawn mower
A fast runner
A fox disliker
A hand biter
A reproducer

What am I?
A rabbit.

Joshua Lathey (11)
Queen's Dyke Primary School

Stone Farm - Cinquains

Classroom
Feeling nervous
I'm going to Stone Farm
Stay strong, be brave, be a grown-up
My life!

Stone Farm
'Bye animals!'
Breakfast was delicious
Pack my bags, I'm so excited
Goodbye!

Christian Olive (11)
Queen's Dyke Primary School

My Adventure At Stone Farm - Cinquains

Be brave
Parents crying
I'll be strong and survive!
Miss family, even my fish
Stay brave!

I'm glad
It's all over
My life has now all changed
Reunited with family
Sleep tight.

Next day
Think of Stone Farm
Remember that fun week
Look up high in the sky and think
Sky high.

Callum Clarke (11)
Queen's Dyke Primary School

Stone Farm - Haikus

Monday
Wake up! Rush to school
Meet my friends, Stone Farm is here
Go on the coach, fun!

Tuesday
Going to the pool
Laughing, splashing and bombing
Having a great time.

Wednesday
Sizzling away
Singing along with people
Having a great time!

Thursday
Looking at the fish
Watching all of them swimming
Having a great time!

Friday
Leaving from Stone Farm
Wave bye to everybody
Here I am at home.

Rebecca Newport (10)
Queen's Dyke Primary School

The Boy From Queen's Dyke School

There was a young boy from Queen's Dyke
Who had a £500 bike
He tempted his fate
Smacked into a gate
That poor young boy from Queen's Dyke.

Ben Kinchin (11)
Queen's Dyke Primary School

The Fierce Monster

He's bright and gives a fright in his predictable way
Can he claim a victim at this time of day?

The umbrella being pushed around like a tornado in the air
She is praying and hoping for someone to care.

The rain ripping through the black almighty clouds
Thumping on the houses' wooden heads all aloud.

The scarecrow being pushed over with terror on his face
This is a grave moment, the end of the scarecrow race.

The dead tree is a badge of honour for the monster dead on the floor
This lonely badge of honour is dead no more.

The house is fiercely scarred
Where the lightning hit ferociously hard, hard, hard.

This criminal can kill, he is dangerous without a doubt
So I warn you, we are not all safe from this monster, so

Watch out!

Owen Churchill (11)
Queen's Dyke Primary School

The Famous Death

Swipes through the ocean big and bold,
Until she hits an iceberg cold.

The puffs of smoke fogging the view,
The lookouts cannot see the clear deep blue
The unsinkable ship is . . .
Sinking,
Sinking,
Sinking,

The unsinkable ship sailing night and day,
Hits something blocking her on her watery way.

She is gliding through the water, like a wedded bride,
Sailing softly, silently, active, keeping her pride.

She is . . .
Sinking,
Sinking,
Sinking,

Her bones are breaking, blending with the black clear sky,
Cracking, groaning, screeching like bonfire Guys.

She has now . . .
Sunk,
Sunk,
Sunk,

It is done and she has gone to her icy grave
Where she will live, rot and no longer be brave.

Adina Gibbard (11)
Queen's Dyke Primary School

The Sea - Cinquains

Horrid
Fast and flowing
Muddy, don't go in there
Sticks, stones, leaves, seaweed not glowing
Horrid!

The sea
Slowly flowing
Clean fishes swimming slow
Glowing in the moonlight, sparkling
Shining.

Chloë Dunseath (11)
Queen's Dyke Primary School

The Lonely Person

He shouts to the birds
With his powerful words.

'Shoo, shoo, go away!'
For he stays there 24 hours a day.

I am in the golden fields all alone
In the distance I hear a tone.

It's the farmer in his truck
Would this be my pot of luck?

Bang, bang, bang, I cry in fear
I don't want the farmer to come near
For he might blow off my ear.

Now I am packed away this season
Maybe I will be back for another reason.

Ashley Ashcroft (11)
Queen's Dyke Primary School

The Destroyers

Walking through the empty street
Looking at his partner's defeat

Causing blackouts in every home
Every river turns to foam

Lighting up the midnight sky
Tell me God, oh why, oh why?

Slashing up the forest thin
Showing that he'll always win

Shouting out his sharp commands
They quickly jump to his demands

Slaughtering the town below
Never feeling any woe

Pitter, patter, on the ground
They're done, there's no more to be found.

Sophie Wright (11)
Queen's Dyke Primary School

What A Life!

There was an old lady from Mars
She lived on chocolate bars
Until one day
She drifted away
Oh, that poor lady from Mars.

Chloe Curtis (11)
Queen's Dyke Primary School

Tooth Picker Kennings

Tooth picker
Gum sticker
Teeth lover
Dirt hater
Ready listener
Knowledge sharer

Who am I?

Michael Long (11)
Queen's Dyke Primary School

Panda Kennings

Bamboo eater
Poacher hater
Food lover
Forest coverer
Black and white
No fighter
Slow breeder
Forest needer

Who am I?

Kyle Frost (10)
Queen's Dyke Primary School

What Am I? Kennings

Wing flapper
Tooth taker
Glitter spreader
Room breaker
Ballet dancer
Midnight prancer
Dress wearer
Magic bearer

One small tooth fairy.

Alicia Scammell (10)
Queen's Dyke Primary School

What Am I? Kennings

Loud roarer
Meat eater
Fast runner
Person hater
Prey taker
Zoo teaser

What am I?

Nick Morse (11)
Queen's Dyke Primary School

Jacket Potato - Haiku

It's taking ages
I am waiting for dinner
Ding! Yes, it's ready.

Georgea Winstone (10)
Queen's Dyke Primary School

Kitten - Haiku

Darting through catflaps
They are furry and funny
Very cute faces!

Ashley Barnes (11)
Queen's Dyke Primary School

Tornado Term - Haiku

Wind whirling surprise
Tearing aged houses down
Ripping through the earth.

Daisy Merriman (10)
Queen's Dyke Primary School

The Dog - Haiku

Dog needed water
But his water bowl was dry
His thirst went unquenched.

Adam Field (10)
Queen's Dyke Primary School

Swim - Haiku

Long, scaly tail, *splash*
Gliding smooth through the water
Swim, swim, sea horse swim!

Chloe Lathey (11)
Queen's Dyke Primary School

Dragon - Haiku

Ancient guardian
Fiery wings blaze gracefully
Through travellers' haze.

Mick Ritchie (10)
Queen's Dyke Primary School

Leaves - Haiku

Leaves fall down lightly
In autumn, softly floating
Spread like a carpet.

Chelsea Anderson (10)
Queen's Dyke Primary School

Stone Farm - Cinquain

Stone Farm
Is in Bridestowe
Mr, Mrs Hatton
Feeding animals on the farm
Yard now.

Euan McGinness (10)
Queen's Dyke Primary School

Robots - Cinquain

Robots
The invasion
Big silver destroyers
Kill the robots! Kill the robots!
Cool game.

Liam Hole (10)
Queen's Dyke Primary School

Kitten - Haiku

The soundless fur sits
Curled quietly on his bed
Why should he wake up?

Callum MacDonald (10)
Queen's Dyke Primary School

There Was An Old Man Of Witney

There was an old man of Witney
Who set off on a journey to Sydney
When he was on the plane
His neighbour was insane
On landing, he was glad to still have his kidney!

Ben Stanley (11)
Queen's Dyke Primary School

The Boy From Queen's Dyke

There was a dull boy from Queen's Dyke
He had an enormous great bike
He glided past the school
And fell in a great big pool
That poor dull boy from Queen's Dyke.

Lewis Manning (10)
Queen's Dyke Primary School

There Was A Monkey From Ghana

There was a monkey from Ghana
Who liked to eat a banana
He swung on the trees
Then fell on his knees
Then he got bit by a piranha!

Ben Hardcastle (10)
Queen's Dyke Primary School

There Were Four Men Playing Pontoon

There were four men playing pontoon
In a very dusty old saloon
One went bust
To the other's disgust
As he floated away on a balloon.

Jordan Maycock (11)
Queen's Dyke Primary School

Stone Farm Monday - Cinquain

The day
I can do it
Be strong, brave and happy
It's only a few days really
Not long.

Carlee Shayler (10)
Queen's Dyke Primary School

The Jungle

Down in the jungle
In the heat
There was a tiger and a leopard
A monkey swung from tree to tree
The leopard crept through the trees
The tiger pounced
Move out of the way!

Nicholas Corrigan (7)
Radley CE School

Puppies

Puppies, puppies,
It's time for your bath
To make you beautiful and clean
And then it's time for dinner too
Then bedtime and you're ready for bedtime too
Goodnight, goodnight, goodnight.

Daisy Stoyle (7)
Radley CE School

Planes, Planes, Planes

Planes are really noisy,
They're like a hummingbird.
They're flying round all day
And they're always being heard.

Planes are really busy,
They're flying all day long.
Some are small and weak
And some are big and strong.

Planes are really deadly,
They're flying round the world.
They're flying up and down
And flying round in twirls.

Sebastian Charles Small (8)
Radley CE School

Football

There was a team called Man City
Whose players ran very quickly,
They went for the goal,
But the ball hit the pole
And put it out for a corner.

The game then went on
And the teams battled strong,
Then the ball hit the post
And went in the goal
So City were now sitting pretty.

City thought they were smart
But they then lost control
And the ball went in the goal
For United.

This now made a draw
With this 1-1 score,
But City were still in
With a chance.

They went up the pitch
And had a great hit
And hooray, it went in
And Man City were 2-1 up.

There was still time to play
With two minutes left,
So the game was still
All to play for.

The ref blew the whistle
And the score was 2-1,
So City had won the game!

Ryan Stubbs (8)
Radley CE School

Coast Rescue

Coastguard Rescue out at sea
While on land, teams in their Jeeps
Race across sandy beaches.

Rescue choppers out on cliffs
Use the winch
Down it goes, with the winchman
Down he goes, the boat gets bigger
Then up he goes to HQ.

Lifeboats rage in stormy seas
In gale force winds of 60 kilometres
The door is open, down he goes at the bottom
Then . . .
Splash!

Samuel Yates (8)
Radley CE School

If I Had A Time Machine

If I had a time machine
I would whiz back to the Triassic period
Triceratops is foraging in the ferns
Brachiosaurus is breaking down branches.

If I had a time machine
I would zoom forward to the future
Where humans live in space pods
And have food that tastes like whatever they want!

If I had a time machine
Egypt is the place for me
I'd be the Pharaoh
And make sure the slaves kept me well.

Could I have a space machine?
If I had a space machine . . .

Conor Mosedale (9)
Radley CE School

Swimmers

Swimmers swimming down the pool
Lifeguards shouting, 'Don't play ball!'
Front crawl, backstroke, breaststroke too,
Underwater fish say, *'Boo!'*

Babies are laughing in the baby pool
The baby pool is very cool
Chlorine is smelly, talcum powder too!
Remember the fish are all saying, *'Boo!'*

The water fountain is going
It makes me all excited
I jump up and down
Until I get quite cold.

The rolling waves are growing
Splish, splash, splosh
Mum shouts, 'Time for tea!'
Oh, my gosh!

Edward Walker (8)
Radley CE School

Flea Limerick

There once was a boy called Lee
Who dreamt he had turned into a flea
He hopped and he hopped
And his parents' jaws dropped
But soon he was stuck in some jelly!

Aoife Lyford (8)
St Mary's RC School, Bicester

SpongeBob Kennings

Bubble blower
Jellyfisher
Patty maker
Patrick lover
Sea sucker
Pineapple dweller.

Jacob Wise (8)
St Mary's RC School, Bicester

Two Little Kittens

Two little kittens, what do they want?
They're miaowing quietly, but what do they want?
It said in letter in very big font,
We want love, that's all we want.

How will we give love?
I have got it!
It will shine right down from above,
So, how do we make it shine from above?
It can't be so complicated, they only want love.

We could try feeding them, that would show love,
We don't have any food for them.
Remember we had a kitten and I had spare food,
I kept it just as it came from above,
That will give them loads of love.

I've got the food, now what my love,
Put it in the bowl and serve,
Here they are, just round the curb,
Serve my dear, quickly serve.

They are mewing quietly, what else do they want?
I don't know, we have to find out.
Bring them to the vet's, he will know,
I'll stay here, you will go.
All right, all right, off I am,
I'll have to take the pussycat in the van.

The vet's saying they ran away,
All they need is care today,
I'll give them care today,
I've got room for them anyway.

Dear, get out the old cat's basket,
I'll get an eating bowl,
With their names all in all,
Right, that's great, we'll have a ball!

Got more eating bowls
We need more food, what shall we do?
To the shop, I'll go too,
Right my dear, get the shoes.

We got the stuff, what's next?
I don't know, just bring them in,
They're happy now, after all, it's not that complicated,
We just give them love, that is all.

Ruth Anne Lazarus (8)
St Mary's RC School, Bicester

The Magic Box
(Based on 'Magic Box' by Kit Wright)

I will put in the box . . .
A stroke of a python's tongue,
The taste of a snowflake,
Landing softly on my tongue.

I will put in the box . . .
Hearing the sound of my baby cousin,
Clapping with his small hands,
Watching a mint choc chip ice cream,
Melting in the yellow sun,
Smelling a bunch of fresh red roses,
Blossoming in the spring.

I will put in the box . . .
Five red roses being picked
Three stone surfboards
Eight golden Victorian rings.

I will put in the box . . .
The taste of my sticky fingers,
After baking cookies,
Hearing 1950's music,
Gazing at the waterfall named Angel Falls.

I will put in the box . . .
Sniffing the salty sea air,
Tasting the home-made birthday cake,
Hearing the birds sing a great tune.

My box is fashioned from . . .
Diamonds and rubies and gems,
With stars on the lid
And a sprinkle of magic from a hand
In the corners.

Maddie Peacey (8)
The Blake CE Primary School

My Magic Box
(Based on 'Magic Box' by Kit Wright)

I will put in my box . . .
The delicious smell of my mummy's cakes,
The touch of a cold shower in the changing room,
The loud sound of thunder and lightning.

I will put in my box . . .
The taste of a warm marshmallow that has been under the fire
And melts when it is in your mouth,
The sound of raindrops pattering on the rooftops,
The twinkle of a star in the night sky.

I will put in my box . . .
Birds flapping their wings in the winter's breeze,
A sweetie from a sweetie-leetie tree,
Freshly made bread that has just come out of the oven.

I will put in my box . . .
A stroke of a soft dog's fur when it has been raining,
The rumble of a dinosaur's tummy when it is hungry,
The scent of a daffodil in the spring.

My box is fashioned from . . .
Gold and steel,
With stars hidden in the corners
And a big star on the lid.
Its hinges are made from sweeties.

Abigail Langley (8)
The Blake CE Primary School

Seasons

The blossom is blue
The sun is rising
The wind falls down like a kite
Summer comes, winter goes
But when the spring comes
It is in-between those.

The winter comes, the summer goes
The trees fall dead, as dead can be
But oh, will I miss you
The summer gave me joy
But now it is time for me to enjoy
The winter that comes before you.

Oliver Moss (9)
The Blake CE Primary School

My Magic Box
(Based on 'Magic Box' by Kit Wright)

I will put in my box . . .
The sound of crashing waves on the beach
The taste of popcorn crackling in your mouth
The smell of freshly made bread.

I will put in my box . . .
The touch of a soft polar bear's fur
A girl smelling a chocolate ice cream
Lightning striking the night sky.

I will put in my box . . .
Fireworks exploding in my garden
Sweetie-tweetie tree
Children screaming and shouting on rides.

I will put in my box . . .
Birds singing on a summer's day
Flowers waving in the breeze
Diamonds glinting in the sun.

My box is fashioned from . . .
Ice, gold and silver
With soft bits on the outside
With the most amazing zigzags
And Curly Wurlys on the lid
In the corners are three wishes

My box is fashioned from . . .
Hinges that are cats' claws.

Imogen Pitson (7)
The Blake CE Primary School

The Moon

The moon lights up
The whole dark sky
Like a light bulb
The moon.

The moon shimmers
Creeps across
The entire night sky
The bright night.

The moon stays
In the middle
Of the sky
Like a pebble.

The moon
Becomes tired
Of standing still
In the centre of the sky
Daylight.

Lewis Denbow (8)
The Blake CE Primary School

God, The Maker

God is the Maker
And I'm the caretaker
Loving and caring is what we need
God is the Maker
And I'm the caretaker
A fair and happy world is what we plead.

God is the Maker
And I'm the caretaker
Education is what we need
God is the Maker
And I'm the caretaker
No war or badness is what we plead.

God is the Maker
And I'm the caretaker
Responsibility is what we need
God is the Maker
And I'm the caretaker
A fabulous life is what we plead.

Abbie Willcox (9)
The Blake CE Primary School

Healthy Living Poem

I love to eat healthily
I think it's great
Carrots, peas and kiwis
Are my best mates

One, two, three, four, five
Eat your five a day
'Or you'll grow fat!'
All mothers say

I've never had a filling
My teeth shine
This is because
I eat fruit all the time

Vegetables and fruit
Are my favourite dinner
Chocolate is the loser
And vegetables are the winner

So, once in a while
Nibble a juicy carrot
Or peck some seeds
Like a healthy parrot!

Georgia Hackett (10)
The Blake CE Primary School

The Magic Box
(Based on 'Magic Box' by Kit Wright)

I will put in my box . . .
A glance of a blazing firework,
The scent of a strong perfume,
Gossip from a teenager spoken in French.

I will put in my box . . .
The tasteless soup my mother gave me,
A book of Ancient Egypt,
The shrieking of an amazed audience.

I will put in my box . . .
Mischievous monkeys making mischief on Monday,
Whistling from a leaf in the autumn breeze,
The sight of baby elephants being showered by their parents.

I will put in my box . . .
The cries of Mary and Joseph for their son, the Son of God,
A fantastic magician making magic,
Mini Coopers rushing through the traffic at 100mph.

My box is fashioned from . . .
Gold and steel and silver,
With hieroglyphics on the lid
And wishes in the corners.
Its hinges are the toe joints of a polar bear.

Katie Steele (8)
The Blake CE Primary School

The Magic Box
(Based on 'Magic Box' by Kit Wright)

I will put in the box . . .
A swish of an eagle swooping down,
The first laugh of an ancient clown,
The twinkle of a star glowing in my eyes.

I will put in the box . . .
A rainbow that goes from England to China,
A sweep from a glider, swooping over my head,
A sip of River Windrush water.

I will put in the box . . .
A lion on a broomstick,
The smell of melting chocolate in the lake
And the smell of burning paper.

Sebastian Ombler (7)
The Blake CE Primary School

The Magic Box
(Based on 'Magic Box' by Kit Wright)

I will put in my box . . .
The sound of a small snorting pig,
On the lid of my box
There are welcomes and stories
From the Wild West.

My box is made from . . .
Sparkling jewels,
The hinges are made from chains
From an ancient drawbridge.

I will travel in my box . . .
To Antarctica.

I will put in my box . . .
The sight of India
Sparkling in the distance.

I will put in my box . . .
The watery taste of pasta with pesto.

I will put in my box . . .
Me, touching a king python.

Freddie Greenan (7)
The Blake CE Primary School

The Magic Box
(Based on 'Magic Box' by Kit Wright)

I will put in the box . . .
The sound of Daleks screaming,
'Exterminate!'
And the TARDIS vanishing
Unbelievably.

My box is fashioned from . . .
Dalekunium
And its hinges are
The Doctor's two hearts
And the Dalek Emperor's mutant
Showing through visible glass.

I will put in the box . . .
The sight of the Mallard
Chugging quickly by
I shall go to Egypt in my box
And see the great sphinx
And the great pyramids
And the sight of my sister's hamster
Doing acrobatics.

William Monahan (7)
The Blake CE Primary School

The Magic Box
(Based on 'Magic Box' by Kit Wright)

I will put in the box . . .
The sound of my cat purring
Sitting on my lap.

I will put in the box . . .
The feel of my cat's cute paws.

I will put in the box . . .
The soft smell of a rose
In your room.

I will put in the box . . .
The taste of chocolate
Melting in your mouth.

I will put in the box . . .
The sound of the waves
Whooshing all day in the sea.

My box is fashioned from . . .
Paint, gold and silver
With flowers on the lid
And messages in the corners.

Its hinges are kittens' cute paws.

I shall canoe on my box
On the great River Windrush
Then wash ashore in a field of horses
Then ride away home
On a beautiful chestnut horse.

Lucy Cox (8)
The Blake CE Primary School

The Magic Box
(Based on 'Magic Box' by Kit Wright)

I will put in the box . . .
The taste of a poppadom on the plate.

I will put in the box . . .
A sun as shiny as gold.

I will put in the box . . .
My best friends Chloe, Georgia and Tori.

I will put in the box . . .
A band of angels singing softly.

I will go to Egypt
To see the River Nile.

Charlotte Stoker (8)
The Blake CE Primary School

My Magic Box
(Based on 'Magic Box' by Kit Wright)

I will put in my box . . .
The quiet sound of a swishing sea
On a starry night.

I will put in my box . . .
The touch of a soft football.

I will put in my box . . .
The taste of a boiling hot pizza.

I will put in my box . . .
The sight of a football getting kicked.

My box is made of . . .
Melted chocolate and marshmallows,
I will surf in my box.

Edward Woods (7)
The Blake CE Primary School

The Magic Box
(Based on 'Magic Box' by Kit Wright)

I will put in my box . . .
Hampton v Witney
Witney scored
Everyone started to scream.

My box is fashioned with . . .
Footballs on the edges
And sparks on the lid.
On the front are skulls
From pirates' heads.

The Crazy Frog on his motorbike
Speeding across the bridge, singing.

I will put in my box . . .
The taste of strawberry ice cream
Melting in my mouth
And it makes me shiver.

The touch of my tooth
When it wobbles.

Jack Booth (7)
The Blake CE Primary School

My Magic Box
(Based on 'Magic Box' by Kit Wright)

I will put in my box . . .
The velvety fur of my rabbit on my lap.

I will put in my box . . .
The taste of a chocolate chip ice cream
Melting in my mouth.

I will put in my box . . .
The smell of a summer's flower
When it is freshly picked.

I will put in my box . . .
The picture of Linds and me
By the lake.

I will put in my box . . .
The dance of a ballerina
Dancing to soft music.

I will put in my box . . .
A triple trifle being topped
With cream.

I will put in my box . . .
My best friend, Lucy.

My box is fashioned from gems
I will fly in my box to Egypt
And see the pyramids and mummies.

Emily Chapman (8)
The Blake CE Primary School

The Magic Box
(Based on 'Magic Box' by Kit Wright)

I will put in the box . . .
The sound of Liverpool fans
Singing 'You'll Never Walk Alone' loudly.

I will put in the box . . .
The sight of my hamster
On his hamster wheel.

My box is fashioned from . . .
Dalekunium
And its hinges are
The Doctor's two hearts
And the Dalek Emperor's mutant
Showing through visible glass.

I will put in the box . . .
The sunny sands of Egypt
I shall see Steven Gerrard in my box
He will sign my Liverpool shirt.

I will put in the box . . .
The taste of chocolate
Melting in my mouth.

I will go to Mars in my box
And see an alien.

Thomas Alty (8)
The Blake CE Primary School

My Birthday

For my birthday, I got . . .
Spotty socks,
Five clocks,
A lollipop,
A pink mop,
Ten birthday cards,
A cake that's hard,
A postcard collection,
Loads of confection,
A rosy rose,
A fake nose!
But best of all
(It's still to come)
A great big hug, from my mum!

Leah Gray (11)
West Kidlington Primary School

When I Win The Lottery . . .

I cannot express how I think it's exquisite
When my nana and grandad come to ours to visit;
My nana so caring, my grandad so funny
Yet, when it gets onto the subject of money,
My grandad turns and says to me,
'When I win the lottery . . .

I'll give two million to my kids and a thousand to theirs
The rest of the money (if you're good) can be shared,
A new television, a holiday to relax,
As well as that wine cabinet from TK Max,
Those retirement flats are expensive, I know
I'll have the cash, so I'll get one even so,
A short trip to Blackpool, now that'll be fun
With big dipper rides and bathing in the sun,
Don't go forgetting the Isle of Man
And where was that place you took me and your nan'?
A king-sized bed, now that *would* be nice
A drink of Bucks Fizz, wouldn't hurt once or twice
And I will be hungrily licking my lips
When for three times a day, I eat steak, egg and chips
And your nana, of course, she must have something
A set of garden tools to do the trimming,
Cutting back the roses and tending to the grass
Will greatly become an enjoyable task.'

My grandad leans back in his chair for a sleep
And so up the stairs I quietly creep
And think of tomorrow, the very next day
I do not need to think what my grandad will say,
For his conversation will eternally be,
About when he wins the lottery . . .

Naomi Heffer (10)
West Kidlington Primary School

Caribbean Beach

The palm of palms, raining coconuts,
Like boulders at your head.
Yet . . .
The palm of palms will shelter you,
Like a loving parent.
Yet . . .
The palm of palms does many things,
It tickles and it waves,
Yet . . . yet . . . yet . . .

                              The tide has come in,
                      Filled with lobsters and crabs.
                                    Just so . . .
                              Splash after splash,
                Tosses out starfish and shrimp alike.
                                      Just so . . .
              Sometimes a wave will be enormous
                        And bearing down on you.
                  Just so . . . just so . . . just so . . .

The ruby-coloured sky,
Reflects in the once sapphire waters.
Gems . . .
The amber sun,
Sinks to a garnet-red.
Gems . . .
The sky then sinks,
To a lapis-like glow.
Gems . . . gems . . . gems . . .

        Yet . . . gems . . . and just so . . . it could only be
                            The Caribbean!

Joshua Reynolds (11)
Wootton by Woodstock CE (Aided) Primary School

Caribbean Beach

The tall palms swaying in the whistling wind
Blue spray from the sea spraying up and around.
Seagulls soaring in the huge, bleak sky
The beach so quiet and blank, no one around, just me.
Just sand, the sea and me, no one to play with
No one at all, not even the fish.
I bet they're having fun out in the ocean chasing boats
I wish I were a dolphin.
No one to pester me or nag at me
I would be free!

Louis Williams (9)
Wootton by Woodstock CE (Aided) Primary School

Caribbean Beach

Stick-like figures scorched by the sunlit sky.

Its withered leaves try to grab you
Like the fingers of an old witch.

The leaves gesture frantically
Asking for help.

The bottle-nosed dolphins glide through
Shades of dark green and sapphire.

The branches wave
Imitating an emotional goodbye.

Luke New (10)
Wootton by Woodstock CE (Aided) Primary School

Caribbean Beach

I wonder at the royal palms and remember the monkey faces
And they will burst into growth
After months at the sapphire sea
I see people going from here to there
With plenty to spare.

William Honey (9)
Wootton by Woodstock CE (Aided) Primary School

Caribbean Beach

The lofty palm rocks in the wind
The palm is as high as an aeroplane in the turquoise sky
When the draught is high, the emerald leaves fall off
And then the tree becomes bare
The strong palm protects you from the gleaming sun.

The top of the tree is as spiky as a porcupine
It keels over and tickles you
The top wiggles about and then all the leaves disappear.

A coconut bops on your head, then rolls into the sea
Like a bowling ball
It floats away into the mist
And slowly cracks open like a pistachio nut
It starts green and when it ripens
It suddenly becomes brown and hairy.

People make giant sandcastles in the golden sand
The tide draws near and washes them away
Looking for shells, but there is nothing in sight.

As the sun goes down
The sea becomes still
And suddenly the moon appears
In the dark, cloudy sky
So we all say goodnight
And goodbye.

Skye Radford (8)
Wootton by Woodstock CE (Aided) Primary School

Caribbean Beach

The silky sea laps over the soft sand
Seagulls gliding overhead
Wave after wave tosses out on me
Travellers playing beach cricket
The boiling sun lashing on my skin

The palm trees protect you like the touch of a loving parent
Keeping you shaded
Watching your every move
Saving you from sunburn
Standing high on their stalks

Palm trees swaying in the breeze
Slapping each other
Shooting coconuts into the sapphire sea
They will float for months
Before bursting into growth

Laying on the beach
Swimming in the blue, warm sea
Building marvellous sandcastles
Covering parents in sand while they're sleeping
These are things I do on the beach.

Ben Capel (10)
Wootton by Woodstock CE (Aided) Primary School#

Caribbean Beach

The big sea, its sapphire colour
It shimmers with light when the sun is shining.
The sandy beaches with the gigantic rocks
When the tide comes in the sea slaps them.

Thomas Ramli-Davies (8)
Wootton by Woodstock CE (Aided) Primary School

Caribbean Beach

Palm trees tall
Palm trees thin
Palm trees spiky
Umbrella leaves
Protecting coconuts from the sun
Good to eat for everyone.

Waves crashing across the shiny sea
Coconuts floating across the shiny sea
Boats smacking coconuts in the sea.

Frank Robert New (8)
Wootton by Woodstock CE (Aided) Primary School

Caribbean Beach

The soundless wind whistling towards the waves
A sandy beach glittering in the sun
The shiny, sandy beach glowing.

The hummingbird hovering harmlessly by a tropical flower
Ready to collect a drink of nectar from among the petals
The giggling monkeys leaping from branch to branch
Shriek and play like baby tree goblins.

On the edge of the sand stands a scarlet ibis
Its curving beak like a gleaming cutlass
Its feathers a bright red ruby.

George Parker (8)
Wootton by Woodstock CE (Aided) Primary School

Caribbean Beach

Sunny, lovely
Yellow ball of fire
Sandy beach
White and smooth stuff.

Finlay Mayo (8)
Wootton by Woodstock CE (Aided) Primary School

Caribbean Beach

The world is enclosed by bright blue skies
Satin sparkles reflect from the glittering waters,
The sea tosses crabs onto the beach
As a frothy wave lunges over the sandy rocks.

The wind comes afterwards
And frightens everyone,
Contracting around us
We have a chance of escaping
The twisting tornado's approaching.

I wonder what can settle the devastation that has left,
Something that shines brightly,
Brighter than the king of kings,
It showers light over the jewelled sand,
It rules the beach.

The palms protect you like the palm of a loving parent
They tickle the tip of your head
When they bend down to make you laugh
They slap others in rapid wind,
They shade you when the giant opal flashes up above.

A giant fire erupts as sunset arrives.

Joshua Ramli-Davies (10)
Wootton by Woodstock CE (Aided) Primary School

Caribbean Beach

Long and bumpy,
Leaves flying in the sky,
Coconuts falling down from the trees.
The coconuts falling, then going into the sea,
Floating in the big, big ocean,
Sinking down and down and down in the dark sea.

Henry Chesterman (7)
Wootton by Woodstock CE (Aided) Primary School

Caribbean Beach

Beautiful birds sing in the nearby trees
While shining waves crash over the beach.
But just offshore, in the deep blue sea
Boats swarm the waves
And all stray fish will get snatched by the ships
And never be seen again.
As the blooming coconuts roll down the beach
Seals watch from a distance.

Peter Moss (9)
Wootton by Woodstock CE (Aided) Primary School

Caribbean Poem

Palm trees with their feathery leaves
Swaying in the light breeze
Palm trees stand way up there
Weighed down by coconut hair

See how I dive deep in the sea
The waves launch me down, one, two, three
Diving down in the sapphire sea
Look at me, I'm full of glee

The clear blue sky is up there
I can feel a little warm air
I see a cloud shaped as a fish
And I make a little wish

Lying down on the golden sand
I feel a shell in my hand
Sand trickles through my toes
That's the way my holiday goes.

Megan Dyer (8)
Wootton by Woodstock CE (Aided) Primary School

Caribbean Beach

Palm trees here with swaying leaves
Dancing in the summer breeze
The watchful palms stand guard over the beach
Like a lifeguard high up on his pole-like chair

Hear the waves overlapping
See the sun shining down
Look at the sunset all lit up
It's just fire in the sky

Searching the sandy beach
For pretty shells
Look, it's pearl-coloured
It's a beautiful shell.

Alexandra Cross (9)
Wootton by Woodstock CE (Aided) Primary School

Caribbean Beach

Sleeping under the bending palm trees
Watching them sway below the scorching sun
Splashing waves go on and on
Approaching the sandy beaches around the world
The sand is wet and dry, creating sandcastles in the sand
Lingering late for the tide to come in
Washing away the sandcastles made.

Molly Capel (8)
Wootton by Woodstock CE (Aided) Primary School

Caribbean Beach

Palm trees are a part of beaches
Gathered together
Like houses in the city
As I hang on the pole-like palms
Nature gathers around me
When they observe the sun-blasted beach
I feel them watching me

The sand feels hot when the sun is flaming
When you walk on it, your feet roast, piping hot
The rocks wash away and turn into sand
Children play, their feet sizzling
Building sandcastles, laughing and playing
Sand crunching, ripening

The sea rippling in the sunny breeze
Waves crashing on the sturdy rocks
The salty scents of the ocean ahead
As I splash in the soggy water
I feel the sand wash away
I love Caribbean beaches!

Calla Cambrey (9)
Wootton by Woodstock CE (Aided) Primary School

Caribbean Beach

The sunny bright sky and bright sun
People sit or lay on deckchairs, talking and eating
Coconuts spread and drop from trees and leaves sway.

Palm trees wave in the wind
The ocean sways with the palm trees
People get blown away by the wind.

Lucy Oliver (7)
Wootton by Woodstock CE (Aided) Primary School

Young Writers Information

We hope you have enjoyed reading this book - and that you will continue to enjoy it in the coming years.

If you like reading and writing poetry drop us a line, or give us a call, and we'll send you a free information pack.

Alternatively if you would like to order further copies of this book or any of our other titles, then please give us a call or log onto our website at
www.youngwriters.co.uk

Young Writers Information
Remus House
Coltsfoot Drive
Peterborough
PE2 9JX

(01733) 890066